This Book Belongs To:

....

....

....

My Personal Information

Name: .... Middle Name: ....

Surname: .... Phone: ....

City: .... State: .... Zip Code: ....

Email: ....

Address: ....

....

....

Place of Birth: .... Date of Birth: ....

Birthmarks: .... Blood Type: ....

Hair Color: .... Eye Color: ....

Driver's Licence Number: ....

Passport Number: ....

National Health Number: ....

National Insurance Number: ....

Social Security Number: ....

Primary Care Physician: ....

Work Information

Work Name: .... Phone: ....

Adress: .... Email: ....

Other Details

Notes For Family Members

List of Important Contacts & People to be Notified

Name:

Relationship:

Email: Phone:

Address:

Name:

Relationship:

Email: Phone:

Address:

Name:

Relationship:

Email: Phone:

Address:

Name:

Relationship:

Email: Phone:

Address:

Name:

Relationship:

Email: Phone:

Address:

Name: ....

Relationship: ....

Email: .... Phone: ....

Address: ....

Name: ....

Relationship: ....

Email: .... Phone: ....

Address: ....

Name: ....

Relationship: ....

Email: .... Phone: ....

Address: ....

Name: ....

Relationship: ....

Email: .... Phone: ....

Address: ....

Name: ....

Relationship: ....

Email: .... Phone: ....

Address: ....

Name:

Relationship:

Email: Phone:

Address:

Name:

Relationship:

Email: Phone:

Address:

Name:

Relationship:

Email: Phone:

Address:

Name:

Relationship:

Email: Phone:

Address:

Name:

Relationship:

Email: Phone:

Address:

Name:
Relationship:
Email: Phone:
Address:

Name:
Relationship:
Email: Phone:
Address:

Name:
Relationship:
Email: Phone:
Address:

Name:
Relationship:
Email: Phone:
Address:

Name:
Relationship:
Email: Phone:
Address:

Name:

Relationship:

Email: Phone:

Address:

Name:

Relationship:

Email: Phone:

Address:

Name:

Relationship:

Email: Phone:

Address:

Name:

Relationship:

Email: Phone:

Address:

Name:

Relationship:

Email: Phone:

Address:

Important Documents & Their Places

Document: .... Location: ....
Note: ....

Document: .... Location: ....
Note: ....

Document: .... Location: ....
Note: ....

Document: .... Location: ....
Note: ....

Document: .... Location: ....
Note: ....

Document: .... Location: ....
Note: ....

Document: .... Location: ....
Note: ....

Document: .... Location: ....
Note: ....

Document: _____ Location: _____
Note: _____

Document: _____ Location: _____
Note: _____

Document: _____ Location: _____
Note: _____

Document: _____ Location: _____
Note: _____

Document: _____ Location: _____
Note: _____

Document: _____ Location: _____
Note: _____

Document: _____ Location: _____
Note: _____

Document: _____ Location: _____
Note: _____

Document: _____ Location: _____
Note: _____

Where You Find My Keys

Key: .... Location: ....
Note: ....

Key: .... Location: ....
Note: ....

Key: .... Location: ....
Note: ....

Key: .... Location: ....
Note: ....

Key: .... Location: ....
Note: ....

Key: .... Location: ....
Note: ....

Key: .... Location: ....
Note: ....

Key: .... Location: ....
Note: ....

Where You Find My
Electronic Devices

Device: .... Location: ....
Note: ....

Device: .... Location: ....
Note: ....

Device: .... Location: ....
Note: ....

Device: .... Location: ....
Note: ....

Device: .... Location: ....
Note: ....

Device: .... Location: ....
Note: ....

Device: .... Location: ....
Note: ....

Where You Find My

Jewerly

Jewerly: .... Location: ....
Note: ....

Jewerly: .... Location: ....
Note: ....

Jewerly: .... Location: ....
Note: ....

Jewerly: .... Location: ....
Note: ....

Jewerly: .... Location: ....
Note: ....

Jewerly: .... Location: ....
Note: ....

Jewerly: .... Location: ....
Note: ....

Jewerly: .... Location: ....
Note: ....

Where You Find My collectibles

Name: .... Location: ....
Note: ....

Name: .... Location: ....
Note: ....

Name: .... Location: ....
Note: ....

Name: .... Location: ....
Note: ....

Name: .... Location: ....
Note: ....

Name: .... Location: ....
Note: ....

Name: .... Location: ....
Note: ....

Name: .... Location: ....
Note: ....

☰ Emails and Social Media Logins ☰

Website: .... | Website: ....
Username: .... | Username: ....
Password: .... | Password: ....
Note: .... | Note: ....

Website: .... | Website: ....
Username: .... | Username: ....
Password: .... | Password: ....
Note: .... | Note: ....

Website: .... | Website: ....
Username: .... | Username: ....
Password: .... | Password: ....
Note: .... | Note: ....

Website: .... | Website: ....
Username: .... | Username: ....
Password: .... | Password: ....
Note: .... | Note: ....

Website: .... | Website: ....
Username: .... | Username: ....
Password: .... | Password: ....
Note: .... | Note: ....

Website: _____ Website: _____
Username: _____ Username: _____
Password: _____ Password: _____
Note: _____ Note: _____

Website: _____ Website: _____
Username: _____ Username: _____
Password: _____ Password: _____
Note: _____ Note: _____

Website: _____ Website: _____
Username: _____ Username: _____
Password: _____ Password: _____
Note: _____ Note: _____

Website: _____ Website: _____
Username: _____ Username: _____
Password: _____ Password: _____
Note: _____ Note: _____

Website: _____ Website: _____
Username: _____ Username: _____
Password: _____ Password: _____
Note: _____ Note: _____

Website: _____ Website: _____
Username: _____ Username: _____
Password: _____ Password: _____
Note: _____ Note: _____

Website: .... Website: ....
Username: .... Username: ....
Password: .... Password: ....
Note: .... Note: ....

Website: .... Website: ....
Username: .... Username: ....
Password: .... Password: ....
Note: .... Note: ....

Website: .... Website: ....
Username: .... Username: ....
Password: .... Password: ....
Note: .... Note: ....

Website: .... Website: ....
Username: .... Username: ....
Password: .... Password: ....
Note: .... Note: ....

Website: .... Website: ....
Username: .... Username: ....
Password: .... Password: ....
Note: .... Note: ....

Website: .... Website: ....
Username: .... Username: ....
Password: .... Password: ....
Note: .... Note: ....

Insurance Information

Provider: ....
Insurance Type: ....
Policy Number: ....
Agent / Contact: ....
Email: ....
Phone: ....
Website: ....

Notes:

Provider: ....
Insurance Type: ....
Policy Number: ....
Agent / Contact: ....
Email: ....
Phone: ....
Website: ....

Notes:

Provider: ....
Insurance Type: ....
Policy Number: ....
Agent / Contact: ....
Email: ....
Phone: ....
Website: ....

Notes:

Provider: ....

Insurance Type: ....

Policy Number: ....

Agent / Contact: ....

Email: ....

Phone: ....

Website: ....

Notes:

Provider: ....

Insurance Type: ....

Policy Number: ....

Agent / Contact: ....

Email: ....

Phone: ....

Website: ....

Notes:

Provider: ....

Insurance Type: ....

Policy Number: ....

Agent / Contact: ....

Email: ....

Phone: ....

Website: ....

Notes:

Provider:	Notes:
Insurance Type:	
Policy Number:	
Agent / Contact:	
Email:	
Phone:	
Website:	

Provider:	Notes:
Insurance Type:	
Policy Number:	
Agent / Contact:	
Email:	
Phone:	
Website:	

Provider:	Notes:
Insurance Type:	
Policy Number:	
Agent / Contact:	
Email:	
Phone:	
Website:	

Other Details

BANKING & FINANCIAL INFORMATION

Bank Account #1

Bank Name: ....
Country: .... City: .... Region: ....
Address: .... Zip code: ....
Phone: ....

Account Name: ....
Account Type: ....
Account Number: ....
Routing Number: ....

Website: ....
Username: ....
Password: ....

Card Number: .... Pin Code: ....
Credit Limit: ....

Card Number: .... Pin Code: ....
Credit Limit: ....

Notes: ....
....
....

Bank Account #2

Bank Name
Country: .... City: .... Region: ....
Address: .... Zip code: ....
Phone: ....

Account Name: ....
Account Type: ....
Account Number: ....
Routing Number: ....

Website: ....
Username: ....
Password: ....

Card Number: .... Pin Code: ....
Credit Limit: ....

Card Number: .... Pin Code: ....
Credit Limit: ....

Notes: ....

Bank Account #3

Bank Name ....
Country: .... City: .... Region: ....
Address: .... Zip code: ....
Phone: ....

Account Name: ....
Account Type: ....
Account Number: ....
Routing Number: ....

Website: ....
Username: ....
Password: ....

Card Number: .... Pin Code: ....
Credit Limit: ....

Card Number: .... Pin Code: ....
Credit Limit: ....

Notes: ....
....
....

Bank Account #4

Bank Name ....

Country: .... City: .... Region: ....

Address: .... Zip code: ....

Phone: ....

Account Name: ....

Account Type: ....

Account Number: ....

Routing Number: ....

Website: ....

Username: ....

Password: ....

Card Number: .... Pin Code: ....

Credit Limit: ....

Card Number: .... Pin Code: ....

Credit Limit: ....

Notes: ....

....

....

Bank Account #5

Bank Name ....
Country: .... City: .... Region: ....
Address: .... Zip code: ....
Phone: ....

Account Name: ....
Account Type: ....
Account Number: ....
Routing Number: ....

Website: ....
Username: ....
Password: ....

Card Number: .... Pin Code: ....
Credit Limit: ....

Card Number: .... Pin Code: ....
Credit Limit: ....

Notes: ....
....
....
....

Bank Account #6

Bank Name ....

Country: .... City: .... Region: ....

Address: .... Zip code: ....

Phone: ....

Account Name: ....

Account Type: ....

Account Number: ....

Routing Number: ....

Website: ....

Username: ....

Password: ....

Card Number: .... Pin Code: ....

Credit Limit: ....

Card Number: .... Pin Code: ....

Credit Limit: ....

Notes: ....

....

....

Bank Account #7

Bank Name ....
Country: .... City: .... Region: ....
Address: .... Zip code: ....
Phone: ....

Account Name: ....
Account Type: ....
Account Number: ....
Routing Number: ....

Website: ....
Username: ....
Password: ....

Card Number: .... Pin Code: ....
Credit Limit: ....

Card Number: .... Pin Code: ....
Credit Limit: ....

Notes: ....
....
....

Bank Account #8

Bank Name

Country: .... City: .... Region: ....

Address: .... Zip code: ....

Phone: ....

Account Name: ....

Account Type: ....

Account Number: ....

Routing Number: ....

Website: ....

Username: ....

Password: ....

Card Number: .... Pin Code: ....

Credit Limit: ....

Card Number: .... Pin Code: ....

Credit Limit: ....

Notes: ....

Bank Account #9

Bank Name ....
Country: .... City: .... Region: ....
Address: .... Zip code: ....
Phone: ....

Account Name: ....
Account Type: ....
Account Number: ....
Routing Number: ....

Website: ....
Username: ....
Password: ....

Card Number: .... Pin Code: ....
Credit Limit: ....

Card Number: .... Pin Code: ....
Credit Limit: ....

Notes: ....
....
....

Bank Account #10

Bank Name ....
Country: .... City: .... Region: ....
Address: .... Zip code: ....
Phone: ....

Account Name: ....
Account Type: ....
Account Number: ....
Routing Number: ....

Website: ....
Username: ....
Password: ....

Card Number: .... Pin Code: ....
Credit Limit: ....

Card Number: .... Pin Code: ....
Credit Limit: ....

Notes: ....
....
....

Other Details

Credit Cards:

Card Name:

Card Type: .... Bank Name: ....

Card Number: .... Phone Number: ....

Expiry Date: .... Website: ....

Security Code: .... Username: ....

Credit Limt: .... Password: ....

Notes:

Card Name:

Card Type: .... Bank Name: ....

Card Number: .... Phone Number: ....

Expiry Date: .... Website: ....

Security Code: .... Username: ....

Credit Limt: .... Password: ....

Notes:

Card Name:

Card Type: .... Bank Name: ....

Card Number: .... Phone Number: ....

Expiry Date: .... Website: ....

Security Code: .... Username: ....

Credit Limt: .... Password: ....

Notes:

Card Name:

Card Type: .... Bank Name: ....

Card Number: .... Phone Number: ....

Expiry Date: .... Website: ....

Security Code: .... Username: ....

Credit Limt: .... Password: ....

Notes:

Card Name:

Card Type: _____ Bank Name: _____

Card Number: _____ Phone Number: _____

Expiry Date: _____ Website: _____

Security Code: _____ Username: _____

Credit Limt: _____ Password: _____

Notes:

Card Name:

Card Type: _____ Bank Name: _____

Card Number: _____ Phone Number: _____

Expiry Date: _____ Website: _____

Security Code: _____ Username: _____

Credit Limt: _____ Password: _____

Notes:

Card Name:

Card Type: .... Bank Name: ....

Card Number: .... Phone Number: ....

Expiry Date: .... Website: ....

Security Code: .... Username: ....

Credit Limt: .... Password: ....

Notes:

Card Name:

Card Type: .... Bank Name: ....

Card Number: .... Phone Number: ....

Expiry Date: .... Website: ....

Security Code: .... Username: ....

Credit Limt: .... Password: ....

Notes:

Card Name:

Card Type: .... Bank Name: ....

Card Number: .... Phone Number: ....

Expiry Date: .... Website: ....

Security Code: .... Username: ....

Credit Limt: .... Password: ....

Notes:

Card Name:

Card Type: .... Bank Name: ....

Card Number: .... Phone Number: ....

Expiry Date: .... Website: ....

Security Code: .... Username: ....

Credit Limt: .... Password: ....

Notes:

Other Details

Investment

Firm/Institution: ....

Account: .... Email: ....

Username: .... Password: ....

Website: .... Phone: ....

Notes:

Firm/Institution: ....

Account: .... Email: ....

Username: .... Password: ....

Website: .... Phone: ....

Notes:

Firm/Institution: ....

Account: .... Email: ....

Username: .... Password: ....

Website: .... Phone: ....

Notes:

Firm/Institution: ....

Account: .... Email: ....

Username: .... Password: ....

Website: .... Phone: ....

Notes:

Firm/Institution: ....

Account: .... Email: ....

Username: .... Password: ....

Website: .... Phone: ....

Notes:

Firm/Institution: ....

Account: .... Email: ....

Username: .... Password: ....

Website: .... Phone: ....

Notes:

Firm/Institution: ....

Account: .... Email: ....

Username: .... Password: ....

Website: .... Phone: ....

Notes:

Firm/Institution: ....

Account: .... Email: ....

Username: .... Password: ....

Website: .... Phone: ....

Notes:

Firm/Institution: ....

Account: .... Email: ....

Username: .... Password: ....

Website: .... Phone: ....

Notes:

Firm/Institution: ....

Account: .... Email: ....

Username: .... Password: ....

Website: .... Phone: ....

Notes:

Firm/Institution: ....

Account: .... Email: ....

Username: .... Password: ....

Website: .... Phone: ....

Notes:

Firm/Institution: ....

Account: .... Email: ....

Username: .... Password: ....

Website: .... Phone: ....

Notes:

Firm/Institution: ....

Account: .... Email: ....

Username: .... Password: ....

Website: .... Phone: ....

Notes:

Firm/Institution: ....

Account: .... Email: ....

Username: .... Password: ....

Website: .... Phone: ....

Notes:

Firm/Institution: ....

Account: .... Email: ....

Username: .... Password: ....

Website: .... Phone: ....

Notes:

Firm/Institution: ....

Account: .... Email: ....

Username: .... Password: ....

Website: .... Phone: ....

Notes:

Firm/Institution: ....

Account: .... Email: ....

Username: .... Password: ....

Website: .... Phone: ....

Notes:

Firm/Institution: ....

Account: .... Email: ....

Username: .... Password: ....

Website: .... Phone: ....

Notes:

Other Details

Other Details

Bills & Debts

Bills

Who	What for	Amount	Contact

Notes:

Who	What for	Amount	Contact

Notes:

Who	What for	Amount	Contact

Notes:

Who	What for	Amount	Contact

Notes:

Who	What for	Amount	Contact

Notes:

Who	What for	Amount	Contact

Notes:

Bills

Who	What for	Amount	Contact

Notes:

Who	What for	Amount	Contact

Notes:

Who	What for	Amount	Contact

Notes:

Who	What for	Amount	Contact

Notes:

Who	What for	Amount	Contact

Notes:

Who	What for	Amount	Contact

Notes:

Bills

Who	What for	Amount	Contact

Notes:

Who	What for	Amount	Contact

Notes:

Who	What for	Amount	Contact

Notes:

Who	What for	Amount	Contact

Notes:

Who	What for	Amount	Contact

Notes:

Who	What for	Amount	Contact

Notes:

Bills

Who	What for	Amount	Contact

Notes:

Who	What for	Amount	Contact

Notes:

Who	What for	Amount	Contact

Notes:

Who	What for	Amount	Contact

Notes:

Who	What for	Amount	Contact

Notes:

Who	What for	Amount	Contact

Notes:

Bills

Who	What for	Amount	Contact

Notes:

Who	What for	Amount	Contact

Notes:

Who	What for	Amount	Contact

Notes:

Who	What for	Amount	Contact

Notes:

Who	What for	Amount	Contact

Notes:

Who	What for	Amount	Contact

Notes:

Other Details

Debt & Libilities

What	Where to fond the paperwork	Contact	Notes

Debt & Libilities

What	Where to fond the paperwork	Contact	Notes

Debt & Libilities

What	Where to fond the paperwork	Contact	Notes

Debt & Libilities

What	Where to fond the paperwork	Contact	Notes

Debt & Libilities

What	Where to fond the paperwork	Contact	Notes

Other Details

Money I am Owed

Who	What for	Amount	Contact

Notes:

Who	What for	Amount	Contact

Notes:

Who	What for	Amount	Contact

Notes:

Who	What for	Amount	Contact

Notes:

Who	What for	Amount	Contact

Notes:

Who	What for	Amount	Contact

Notes:

Money I am Owed

Who	What for	Amount	Contact

Notes:

Who	What for	Amount	Contact

Notes:

Who	What for	Amount	Contact

Notes:

Who	What for	Amount	Contact

Notes:

Who	What for	Amount	Contact

Notes:

Who	What for	Amount	Contact

Notes:

Money I am Owed

Who	What for	Amount	Contact

Notes:

Who	What for	Amount	Contact

Notes:

Who	What for	Amount	Contact

Notes:

Who	What for	Amount	Contact

Notes:

Who	What for	Amount	Contact

Notes:

Who	What for	Amount	Contact

Notes:

Money I am Owed

Who	What for	Amount	Contact

Notes:

Who	What for	Amount	Contact

Notes:

Who	What for	Amount	Contact

Notes:

Who	What for	Amount	Contact

Notes:

Who	What for	Amount	Contact

Notes:

Who	What for	Amount	Contact

Notes:

Money I am Owed

Who	What for	Amount	Contact

Notes:

Who	What for	Amount	Contact

Notes:

Who	What for	Amount	Contact

Notes:

Who	What for	Amount	Contact

Notes:

Who	What for	Amount	Contact

Notes:

Who	What for	Amount	Contact

Notes:

Other Details

Significant Possessions

Real Estate Information

Property Name	1-	2-
Owners		
Address		
Mortgage Co		
Property Cost		
Amount Owed		
Mortagage Company Phone		
Notes		

Property Name	3-	4-
Owners		
Address		
Mortgage Co		
Property Cost		
Amount Owed		
Mortagage Company Phone		
Notes		

Real Estate Information

	5-	6-
Property Name		
Owners		
Address		
Mortgage Co		
Property Cost		
Amount Owed		
Mortagage Company Phone		
Notes		

	7-	8-
Property Name		
Owners		
Address		
Mortgage Co		
Property Cost		
Amount Owed		
Mortagage Company Phone		
Notes		

Real Estate Information

	9-	10-
Property Name		
Owners		
Address		
Mortgage Co		
Property Cost		
Amount Owed		
Mortagage Company Phone		
Notes		

	11-	12-
Property Name		
Owners		
Address		
Mortgage Co		
Property Cost		
Amount Owed		
Mortagage Company Phone		
Notes		

Real Estate Information

Property Name	13-	14-
Owners		
Address		
Mortgage Co		
Property Cost		
Amount Owed		
Mortagage Company Phone		
Notes		

Property Name	15-	16-
Owners		
Address		
Mortgage Co		
Property Cost		
Amount Owed		
Mortagage Company Phone		
Notes		

Real Estate Information

Property Name	17-	18-
Owners		
Address		
Mortgage Co		
Property Cost		
Amount Owed		
Mortagage Company Phone		
Notes		

Property Name	19-	20-
Owners		
Address		
Mortgage Co		
Property Cost		
Amount Owed		
Mortagage Company Phone		
Notes		

Other Details

Other Details

Vehicle Registration Information

Vehicle Name:

Year:	Month:
S/N:	Reg. No:
Reg. Date:	Exp. Date:
Vehicle Type:	Plate No:
Manufacturer:	Model:
Engine Size:	Engine No:
Owner's Name	
Address	
Phone No:	Email:

Notes:
....
....
....
....
....
....
....

Vehicle Registration Information

Vehicle Name:

Year:	Month:
S/N:	Reg. No:
Reg. Date:	Exp. Date:
Vehicle Type:	Plate No:
Manufacturer:	Model:
Engine Size:	Engine No:
Owner's Name	
Address	
Phone No:	Email:

Notes:

Vehicle Registration Information

Vehicle Name:

Year:	Month:
S/N:	Reg. No:
Reg. Date:	Exp. Date:
Vehicle Type:	Plate No:
Manufacturer:	Model:
Engine Size:	Engine No:
Owner's Name	
Address	
Phone No:	Email:

Notes:
....
....
....
....
....
....

Vehicle Registration Information

Vehicle Name:

Year:	Month:
S/N:	Reg. No:
Reg. Date:	Exp. Date:
Vehicle Type:	Plate No:
Manufacturer:	Model:
Engine Size:	Engine No:
Owner's Name	
Address	
Phone No:	Email:

Notes:
....

....

....

....

....

Other Details

My Funeral Wishes

My Last Days

If on life support, please:

☐ Keep me on indefinitely
☐ Unplug me after ....

....

....

If slowly dying, please:

☐ Take me home   ☐ Leave me in hosptial
☐ Other ....

....

What message would you like to leave:

....

....

....

....

....

Memorial & Burial

Name of Funeral Home: _____

Street Address: _____

City: _____ State: _____ Phone: _____

Interement

Address for internment of casket or urn:

_____

_____

☐ Burial   Casket required: ○ Yes ○ No

Notes: _____

☐ Cremation   Urn required: ○ Yes ○ No

Notes: _____

_____

Where I would like the funeral/memorial service to be held:

_____

_____

Cemetery: _____

Scattered Ashes: _____

Memorial Stone: _____

Clothing Choices for the Deceased

Shirt/Dress: ....

Pants: ....

Shoes: ....

Jewelry: ....

Memorial Service:

Speakers	Pallberers
....	....
....	....
....	....
....	....
....	....
....	....

Place: ....

Music: ....

Readings: ....

Open Casket Desires: ....

Notes:

Other Details

Other Details

My Personal Wishes

Obituary

Letters to Loved Ones

My Apologies

Expression of Gratitude

Final Words

Notes

Signature

Made in the USA
Monee, IL
15 March 2023

29975737R00061